d
dragon
dolphin
duck
dog
digger
dinosaur

The **d**og **d**igs
in the garden.

The **d**igger **d**igs
in the ground.

The **d**uck **d**ives
into the pool.

The **d**inosaur **d**ives into the lake.

The **d**olphin **d**ances
on the sea.

The dragon dances
in the moonlight.

I **d**id, I **d**id, I **d**id—
I **d**id my work today.
I **d**id my work today,
and now it's time to play.